Daring Mighty Things—

The Simplest Way to Start Your First (or Next) New Business.

By

John S. Wren, MBA+
960 Grant St. #727
Denver, CO 80203
www.johnwren.com
(303)861-1447
John@JohnWren.com

1st edition published June, 1993
Current Draft-2nd Edition

December 8, 2009

This is the current text of the 2nd edition my little book on business startup. It was first self-published in 1993 with several printings. Until a couple of years ago, I sold it through local Denver book stores, had lots of positive feedback from readers, never a complaint. A version of this revised edition was serialized and published in the Denver Herald Dispatch Newspaper in 2003.

Amar Bhide, Ph.D., Professor of Entrepreneurship at Columbia University (**http://www.bhide.net/**) has said of the first edition "This is a very useful book for anyone who is starting a new business. I recommend it." Dr. Bhide has recently been called the "new Malcomb Gladwell" because of his recent new book, The Venturesome Economy.

The title ***Daring Mighty Things*** comes from Teddy Roosevelt:

"Far better is it to dare mighty things, to win glorious triumphs, even though checkered by failures, than to rank with those poor spirits who neither enjoy much nor suffer much because they live in the gray twilight that knows neither victory nor defeat."

Your feedback and suggestions as I continue the revision process prior to publication would be appreciated. I'm especially interested in hearing from entrepreneurs who would be willing to have me share their startup stories in the 3rd revised edition after this 2nd edition is published.

Introduction

My name is John. I'm a recovering MBA.

I say I'm a recovering MBA, because much of what I learned in graduate business school is deadly for entrepreneurs. Especially toxic to the success of a start-up is the big business approach to strategic planning, market research, and financing.

There are many books about how to write a business plan. These thick, complex tomes pontificate at the little guy just getting started; they seem to do more harm than good. And, there are lots of books about how to improve the operations of a business once the first few customers are sold. This little book is different. The focus here is how to get started from zero.

I believe that reading this little book would have saved me hundreds of thousands of dollars and a failed marriage. It is based on: 1) my direct experience working in a family business and as an entrepreneur who has started seven businesses; 2) the experience of hundreds of my consulting clients; and 3) the experience of members of organizations I founded--the IDEA Café, groups for people starting new projects, careers, businesses, or campaigns that I first organized in 1994; and Franklin Circles, peer support groups for entrepreneurs and small business owners that I first organized in 1996. And this experience is confirmed by the research findings of Dr. Amar Bhide www.bhide.net.

This little book has two goals: 1) To help you start your first or next new business, and 2) To encourage established entrepreneurs to stimulate their own creativity by mentoring a new entrepreneur. It may also be helpful to you in starting a new project, career, or campaign.

All books are flawed. Teachers teach what they most need to know. That's why I suggest a system of filtering what is said in this book through your own mind, possibly with the help of another entrepreneur who serves as your mentor, and that you join or form a group of others who are starting new businesses in a Franklin Circle or similar group.

John S. Wren, MBA+

The world needs your new business!

To understand my system for starting your new business, it is necessary to first appreciate the nature of business in a capitalistic, free market economy.

The world will always have government, big-business, and big-labor: government for those things individuals cannot do for themselves and big-business and big-labor because of certain efficiencies of scale. Unfortunately, the large scale of these three forms of bureaucratic operations leads to problems:

1) Efficiency comes at the expense of intelligence and creativity. The large organization has a tendency to get better and better at doing what eventually is the wrong thing.

2) Power corrupts. Governmental corruption is kept in check by our process of representative democracy. Big-business corruption is kept in check to the extent that the free market is allowed to operate. That is why big business hates competition.

The world view of the bureaucrat is necessarily different from that of the entrepreneur. The steps recommended here for starting a new business will not make sense to most bureaucrats.

If you decide to work with a business mentor, it is important that you work with someone who subscribes to the following philosophy of business. This person almost always will be an independent business owner.

Beware of seminars about how to start a new business; the most deadly advice for entrepreneurs comes from bureaucrats, public or private, active or retired.

Yes, the world really does need you to create a new business!

There is always a shortage of entrepreneurs, that's why it pays so well.

This shortage of start-up specialists is caused by two things:

1) The infinite power of the human mind to create new ways to help people; and

2) People's unlimited need for help.

Read today's newspaper. It's easy to see the world needs help. To the entrepreneur, these problems are opportunities in working clothes!

Each human life is a story told by God. The entrepreneur's story is about doing Good Work. Good Work (E.F. Schumacher, Small is Beautiful, 1973) has three qualities:

1) Good Work helps customers by providing a necessary and useful product or service at a price they are willing to pay.

2) Good Work provides an adequate income for the entrepreneur and everyone involved in the business.

3) Good Work provides a path for personal growth. Starting a new business is the best form of adult education!

The word entrepreneur comes from a French word which means "to undertake." The entrepreneur is a person who starts or undertakes and assumes the risk for a new business or enterprise. Entrepreneurship has been the vital catalyst to economic growth derived from three technological revolutions over the last five thousand years:

1) The agricultural revolution, caused by the invention of farming, which led to the first surpluses and the need for organized markets

2) The industrial revolution, caused by the invention of the printing press, which led to mass production and mass marketing

3) The current communications revolution, caused by the invention and continual improvement of telecommunications and the computer, and we have no idea where

it will ultimately lead but we are just getting started!

Each of these technological revolutions created the need for entrepreneurs. New businesses are constantly needed to transform the new technology into new products and services. Because of the recent communications revolution, there are more entrepreneurial opportunities today than ever before.

Theoretically, the alternative mechanism for transforming new technology into new products and services is the planned economy. A benevolent dictator could, in theory, be much more efficient, but because of human nature the planned economy has never worked.

The competition of free market capitalism keeps any one person from becoming too powerful. History has demonstrated repeatedly that power corrupts. Despite its inefficiencies, competition provides more consumer benefits that the potentially efficient, planned system.

The planned system concentrates power and eventually corruption grows to the point that the system fails. In the free world, corruption is weeded out through the mechanisms of free market capitalism and representative democracy.

Is there really room for another entrepreneur in the world? Yes! There are an infinite number of possible new businesses. The illusion of scarcity of opportunity is created by some bureaucratic economists. As Kenneth Bolding, a right-minded economist who taught at the University of Colorado told me, "The problem is the economist's pie-chart. There is no pie; there is just a bunch of damned little tarts!"

Disorder and Chaos-the Free Market Environment

The primary conditions that an entrepreneur finds in a free market economy are: friction, uncertainty, constant change, and disorder. The market is messy. Business is war.

Study the *U.S. Marine Corps Book of Strategy* (Warfighting, Currency Books, 1994). It suggests that victory in this sort of messy environment depends on character-intelligence, will, courage, the ability to take action under conditions of uncertainty, honesty, and strength of purpose.

The primary condition in business is friction. Friction is that which makes the simple difficult. Starting a new business with the approach outlined in this book is simple but very difficult.

Few people encourage a new entrepreneur. Relatives and friends are often afraid to offer encouragement because of their own fear of failure. Competitors usually do not give comfort or encouragement to a new competitor because of the fear of lost business.

The best market research can be misleading, and most new entrepreneurs cannot afford the best. It is a myth that people can accurately tell you whether or not they will buy your product or service; smart salespeople know that buyers are liars.

The only way to know if your product or service is going to sell is to sell it. Get to the market quickly. This is simple but very difficult. The opportunity that exists for you today may disappear in just a few weeks. If you see an opportunity, hundreds of others are probably seeing the same

14

thing. Just as in war, there are the quick and there are the dead.

If you are unwilling or cannot make your first sale quickly with your personal resources, think of some other product or service, possibly related to your current idea. For example, publish and promote a newsletter or book instead of starting a consulting firm. Or, get a job in the direction of your dreams, waiting for the next opportunity as you continue to prepare. Timing is everything.

Sooner or Later, You Will Be an Entrepreneur.

With the downsizing of large corporations, we are now experiencing, nearly everyone will eventually be an entrepreneur. Charles Handy (*The Age of Paradox*, Harvard University Press, 1994) was the first to observe that the world economy is restructuring into a shamrock with three leaves: core businesses with a very small central management that outsource nearly all work; millions of small businesses that provide goods and services to the core businesses and to each other; and temporary workers provided through agencies.

Looking back, historians may very well call this The Age of the Entrepreneur. A Gallup Survey found that 70 of high school students want to eventually own and operate their own business. Yet, many people still plod along in jobs they hate.

I suppose some people get trapped by the allure of the high paying corporate jobs that we read about in the newspapers, CEOs who earn millions of dollars a year. But how many of those big jobs are there? Not very many. Climbing the corporate ladder is like buying a ticket in a long-term

lottery. Invest your life and wait 20
years. Someone will win, but it
probably won't be you or me.

Most new ideas don't work, and luck is
a big factor in any success. In a free
market economy, the cost to society of
any one failure is kept low because
the free market encourages millions of
entrepreneurs to take many small
chances. Entrepreneurs take the risk
because:

1) They want to make their work
soulful (Thomas More, Care of the
Soul, 1992) and they have a passion
for their product or service. The
psychological profile of the soulful
entrepreneur is about the same as
that of a Peace Corp volunteer.

Or

2) The entrepreneur has a burning
desire to take their product or service

to the marketplace and the boss just won't listen.

Or

3) They want to make money. Most affluent people are self-employed business owners (Thomas J. Stanley, Networking with the Affluent, 1993). Many entrepreneurs have started because they eventually realized they were doing all the work and their boss was making all the money.

The risk of being an entrepreneur is much less than the risk of betting on a corporate or government career. The corporation or government can steal your soul with meaningless work and then terminate employment just before retirement. The entrepreneur controls his or her own destiny to a much greater extent.

The failure statistics for new businesses are misleading. A close examination shows that many of what are usually counted as failures in the statistics are actually a success for the entrepreneur. Often the "failure" is a stepping stone, preparation for the next new business.

When you hit a dead-end, adjust your objective and goals, then get to your next sale. This may be a job in the direction of your dreams. Getting a job at a coffee shop is the best training for starting a coffee shop. (See ***Bounce! Failure, Resiliency, and Confidence to Achieve Your Next Great Success,*** Barry J. Moltz, Wiley, 2008 and the classic ***What Color is Your Parachute***, Richard Nelson Bolles, Ten Speed Press, 2009 is radically revised and updated, if you haven't read the current edition, you haven't really read it!)

Finding a job is easy for entrepreneurs; corporations want people who are proven entrepreneurs!

Tom Peters (*Tom Peters Seminar-Crazy Times Call for Crazy Organizations,* Vintage Books, 1994) says, "Imagination is the source of value in the economy. It's an insane world, and in an insane world, sane organizations make no sense." Peters encourages companies to make every employee an entrepreneur. You'll fit right in!

The Truth about How to Start Your Own Business

The Small Business Administration (SBA) propaganda and many bureaucrats posturing as new-business consultants say it is necessary to have a written business plan to be successful. Yet, successful entrepreneurs almost never have a formal, written plan before the first sale in their new business.

"Entrepreneurs have to resist the temptation of endless investigation and trust their judgment," says start-up expert Dr. Amar Bhide. "How Entrepreneurs Craft Strategies that Work," written by Dr. Bhide and published in Harvard Business Review, March-April 1994 may be the best short article ever written about the start-up process. It makes a strong case for the start-up approach suggested by me here: creativity and decisive execution.

If you don't know enough to skip market research and strategic planning, you are picking the wrong business. Pick a business that you already know inside and out because of your work experience or your experience as a customer.

Businesses, like everything else in nature, go through three stages: inception, growth, and decline. Anyone who has taken a business course is familiar with the sigmoid curve, the s-shaped line that is used to represent this process.

The key to success in starting a new business is to get to the first sale as quickly as possible. Growth occurs as the methods used to create his first sale are perfected and used as a cookie cutter to create growth.

Eventually, new technology and new competitors will bring companies to a natural end if they don't recreate themselves during good times. The key to continued growth is the ability and willingness to reinvent the business. This process can be represented as a second sigmoid. Andy Grove, President of Intel in his book "Only the Paranoid Survive" calls this the inflection point. He says, "A strategic inflection point occurs when change is so powerful that it fundamentally alters the way business is done." See

I've identified four phases on the path toward starting your first or next business with as little risk as possible, and to then foster your business's continued success by working with a new entrepreneur to stimulate your own creativity.

The four phases of business start-up are:

Phase I-Open your mind to becoming an entrepreneur.

Phase II-Prepare to be in business.

Phase III-Be in business, just do it!

Phase IV-Keep growing or die.

Phase I-Open your mind to becoming an entrepreneur.

You have probably already decided to go into business for yourself (or to grow your business by mentoring a new entrepreneur) or you would not have read this far. But if you are still on the fence, or if you want ideas about what to suggest for your family, friends, and business associates who are undecided, here are some ways to get enthused about owning your own business:

A) Pick the right "parents."

My dad told me he made the decision to be an entrepreneur when his aunt told him, "Whatever you do, be in business for yourself, even if you just own a popcorn stand!" And, of course, I made my decision based on encouragement from my dad. Very often entrepreneurs have a parent, other relative or close friend who is self-employed.

B) Associate with entrepreneurs.

If all your family and friends are all government and big-business bureaucrats, it will be more difficult for you to start your own business unless you make up for this short coming by developing a network of support for yourself. Keep your eyes open for entrepreneurs. When you meet one, try to have lunch and pick his or her brain. Most entrepreneurs love to talk about how they got started.
Eventually, you will meet an entrepreneur who is willing to be your mentor.

A good place to find entrepreneur friends can be one of the weekly meetings of the IDEA Café, see **http://ideacafe.meetup.com/1**. I held the first meeting of what is now called IDEA Café in 1994. It provides a weekly gathering where new entrepreneurs and small business owners can meet and learn from each other. Too far from Denver? Wrong time for you? Start an IDEA Café! Contact me if you want help.

For ongoing support of your growth as an entrepreneur, consider starting or joining a Franklin Circle. The format of each meeting is based on the first group started by Ben Franklin in 1727. Franklin called it "the best school" and Training Magazine agrees with Franklin's judgment of what may have been his best invention. To learn more, attend and IDEA Café meeting, or see my website, **http://www.johnwren.com/**.

C) Practice green light thinking.

Our society places a high value on analytical or red light thinking. The elementary and secondary education system in this country, both public and private, tends to do a good job of teaching it and pounding green light, creative thinking out of us. The child comes into kindergarten with natural sense of curiosity and creativity and leaves 12 years later with much of it lost.

Rekindle your own creative, green light thinking. Read books on creativity. Attend the IDEA Café, or even better start a new one! A good new book on creativity is *The Back of the Napkin. Solving Problems and Selling Ideas with Pictures*, Dan Roam, Portfolio/Penguin, 2008

Become involved with the arts. Take a vacation. Get excited about life and all the possibilities! You no longer have to just sit in your seat and do your work like you did for the first 12 years of school!

The ongoing process of adult learning is critical to your ongoing success as an entrepreneur. Always take time to smell the roses!

Creative green light thinking in all fields comes from having adequate leisure time. Sometimes the best thing you can do for your self and your business is to take a day off and share some time with God.

Phase II-Prepare to be in business.

You may already be prepared to start your own business. The marker that indicates you are ready to go to Phase III, start-up, is having a clear objective and set of goals for getting your first check from a satisfied customer.

Depending on where you are now, you may be in the hunt in the next few days, or you may need to take several months or longer to prepare.

If you already have your first sale, this book can be a useful way for you to continue your own growth by sharing what you've learned with a new entrepreneur (see Phase IV). Here are suggested steps to prepare you for going into business:

KNOW YOURSELF.

What do you really want to do? The better you understand yourself, the more likely you will be to pick the business that is right for you. But don't get stuck; none of us ever achieve absolute self-knowledge. You will learn all kinds of things about yourself as you start your new business, and you can always change the direction of your new business or start over.

You may find that a personal journal is a useful tool in sorting out who you are and what you want to do. Also useful are many of the classes, seminars, groups, and therapy techniques. For the last couple of years I've attended a Socrates Café and have found it very helpful, see **http://socratescafe.meetup.com/** and **http://www.philosopher.org/**.

GET AN ENTREPRENER MENTOR. (In the first edition of this guide, I called this person a coach, a word that has changed its meaning since Coach-U started teaching therapists how to market themselves to business people.)

A good E-mentor shares experience and listens as you clarify your own thinking. A good E-mentor does NOT try to do your thinking for you! One good way to find an E-mentor is to use your network of friends and relatives to identify a successful business owner who might be willing to work with you. The IDEA Café can be a good place to develop new business friendships that can lead to your E-mentor. Or you may want to hire a business consultant to work with you.

If you work with a paid consultant as your E-mentor, make sure he or she has started a business other than his or her consulting practice, and that he or she understands the process of working with new entrepreneurs described here. Ask the potential E-mentor to read this book (if he or she has not already done so) and to give you their opinion of this startup approach before you agree to a second meeting.

Make sure your coach is optimistic and affirming, sincerely wants you to do well, and has good practical common sense. Husbands and wives have been E-mentors to some of the most successful people in history.

Other spouses have ruined careers with their constant nagging and second-guessing.

Have a clear understanding with your coach about how you will work together. If you pick a bad E-mentor, fire him or her and try again. Or go it alone. It is better to have no coach at all than to be hobbled by a bad one.

BECOME A LIFELONG LEARNER.

Approach being an entrepreneur as you would any other profession. Learn as much as you can in whatever way is most helpful to you. Talk with people, read, and attend classes. Invest in your primary asset, yourself. One powerful way to learn more is to join or start a Franklin Circle; it worked for Ben in 1727, maybe it will help you! (For more about Franklin Circles email me at John@JohnWren.com with "Franklin Circles" in the subject line.)

Study alone will not teach you enough.
Every industry has its own secrets,
things you'll never discover just taking
classes and reading books. Get a job
in an industry related to your interests
before you risk your money. Even low-
paying temporary work or volunteer
work can supply the learning needed
to launch your new business. Again,
the best way to learn how to start a
coffee shop is to work in a coffee
shop.

BEWARE OF BAD INFORMATION.

Fred Smith, who started Federal
Express, is sometimes held up as an
example of the power of business
planning and raising venture capital.
The myth is that he wrote a paper at
Yale about his vision for Fed Ex and
then raised several million in venture
capital to get started. That's true as far
as it goes, but it leaves out some very
vital information.

Here is the rest of the story: 1) Smith also started a successful record company when he was fifteen, 2) Fed Ex grew out of a charter air business Smith started first, and 3) when he was twenty-one he got two things from his father who died when he was four- a letter encouraging him not to become part of the idle rich, and a check for one million dollars. So you can see he did not just write a business plan and raise the money, which is the way the story is often told.

CONTINUE YOUR EDUCATION.

The best preparation for success in business is a good, solid liberal arts education. The study of philosophy, literature, history, language, and abstract science is intended to provide general knowledge and develop general intellectual capacities, both of which increase creativity and enjoyment of life. A liberal arts education also enables and encourages lifelong independent learning, which saves the entrepreneur a fortune in seminar fees and wasted time!

Many successful entrepreneurs do not have a formal education beyond high school. Many, such as George Washington, Benjamin Franklin, and Abraham Lincoln, educated themselves through independent self-directed learning.

To facilitate your own independent self-directed learning, you may want to join with others who are interested in similar topics. Franklin Circles are one way to do this. A great guidebook about leading or joining such a learning group is Malcolm Knowles, ***Self-Directed Learning-A Guide for Learners and Teacher***, Jossey-Bass, 1975.

LEARN TO BE AN OPTIMALIST.

Optimalism is a word coined by Tal Ben-Shahar, author of Happier—Learn the Secrets to Daily Joy and Lasting Fulfillment based on his very popular positive psychology class at Harvard University.
http://www.talbenshahar.com/

Ben-Shahar was surprised when people came to his book signings who were already leading happy lives. So his second book became The Pursuit of Perfect—How to Stop Chasing Perfection and Start Living a Richer, Happier Life.

Optimism, always looking at the sunny side, always trying to perfect one's skills, can result in a miserable life. Recognition of problems, taking action, and being grateful for what we have now are essential ingredients for happiness.

Looking at the positive side of life in a realistic way is a learned skill. If you

don't know how, ask one of your
consistently cheerful friends how they
do it, or read Martin Seligman's
"Learned Optimism", 1991 or see his
website
http://www.authentichappiness.org/
.

**PRACTICE THE MOST IMPORTANT
SKILL OF TOP ENTREPRENEURS--
SELLING.**

Salesmanship has a bad reputation in
our society because of the large
number of clerks and other
bureaucrats who resent the high
earnings of sales people. The truth is,
selling is a vital function in our free
market economy. Nothing happens
until someone sells something. That is
why selling is the highest paid
profession, next to entrepreneurship.

What is selling? Selling is causing
someone to do what is in his own best
interest, but which otherwise he or she

would not do. Selling uses the same techniques of persuasion as the scam or con game. The difference? Selling delivers what is promised.

If you do not know how to sell, learn. Become a student of the profession of selling. Read books and magazines, take classes and seminars, and talk with experienced sales people. But, it is not enough to just study.

To become a tennis player, you cannot just study tennis. You have to play the game. To become a good salesperson, you have to practice selling. Take a job doing telemarketing at night and on weekends. Find a job as a retail sales clerk, or become involved with a multi-level marketing organization. You will receive valuable training and experience, and earn extra money to use a capital in your new business.

If you decide to find a sales job, look for an employer who understands how to train new sales people. Talk with past employees. Beware of the manager who doesn't understand selling and just uses experienced sales people.

Some people say they don't want to be involved in selling; they only want to do marketing. By marketing, these people usually mean advertising and public relations. The brightest advertisers understand that marketing is selling. Advertising is salesmanship in print. And public relations that is not carefully tied to the selling process is just a lot of sound and fury.

ACCUMULATE CAPITAL.

Save money.

In addition to cash, acquire other capital assets for start-up: a home you can use as an office, a good car, and a computer.

It is unlikely that a bank or venture capitalist will make a loan or investment with a new entrepreneur. You may be able to borrow from friends and family, but beware. As one successful entrepreneur has said, "raising money has become a disease. Entrepreneurs are wasting lots of brainpower scheming to raise money." (From Amar Bhide's "Bootstrap Finance: The Art of Start-Ups", Harvard Business Revue, November-December 1992. This excellent article is based on a study of 100 founders of successful businesses. It found that **most start-ups lack all or most of the criteria investors use to identify big winners**: scale, proprietary advantages, well-defined plans, and well-regarded founders.)

Having too much money can be a serious handicap for a new business.

Too much money can lead to complacency and buffering of the business from the reality of the market. Raising money from others locks you into plans that may turn out to be wrong. So, bootstrapping is the best strategy for the first-time entrepreneur.

If you are in the fortunate circumstance of having plenty of cash, invest it in your new business, invest it in yourself, or invest it in helping another new entrepreneur. Or just wait. Take a job in the direction of your dream and wait for the right opportunity.

OBTAIN & MAINTAIN A FIT, READY CONDITION.

The foundation is being fit. An important part of this fitness is spiritual conditioning that connects us with a power greater than ourselves. For me, that means: 1) setting aside some time each day for prayer and meditation, 2) being part of a fellowship that follows a similar program, and 3) meeting with someone from time-to-time to check out progress.

Physical fitness for me means getting at least 20 minutes of exercise on most days, even if it is just taking a long walk. Mental fitness is recognizing insanity when it crops up in my life and then doing something about it. Insanity is doing the same thing again and expecting different results.

Fitness is necessary to get started, and it is necessary to keep going. When I hit the wall and cannot go forward another step, it is time for me to regroup and go back to these basics. Nature forces me to pay attention. God whispers to us with pleasure and shouts to us with pain.

Death is just nature's way of saying to slow down!

GET A JOB IN THE DIRECTION OF YOUR DREAM

If you want to open a restaurant, get a job working in one first. It's no accident that Dave worked in a Kentucky Fried Chicken before he started Wendy's.

Most people can find a good job fast, no matter how bad the economy. Make a list of friends, call, tell them you've decided to go in a new direction, and ask who they know that might need help. Call that person and set an appointment. Doing this got me a job in two days that people work for their entire life, to hear how I did it listen to my podcast "How to Find a Good Job Fast" on www.JohnWren.com.

DEVELOP YOUR MOST VALUABLE ASSET: A CLEAR OBJECTIVE AND SET OF GOALS.

Every business starts with one person's imagination. An idea eventually becomes a clear objective and four or five goals for accomplishing that objective. For most people, this transformation is a messy, painful process.

The core idea for the new business usually comes from work experience. Or it comes from life as a consumer: Hobbies, doing chores around the house, shopping, or playing games. The right idea for you won't require a lot of research because it comes from your direct experience.

Idea minnows that eventually grow into successful businesses are usually found in oceans, not fish-tanks. Researching trends doesn't really help. The trend may be against restaurants, but a particular restaurant at a particular time in a particular place may be a great idea. Work hard, play hard, and watch for the great white minnow.

Screen your ideas quickly. Look for an idea that is easy and cheap to implement and that will result in a profitable business. A profitable business for a new entrepreneur with limited resources has clients who: 1) buy enough on the first sale to create a good profit, and 2) who make repeat purchases. For most first-time entrepreneurs, this means you will be selling to businesses, or forming strategic alliances that help you make the connection with the consumer.

A good final screen for your idea is to buy an hour of time from a good CPA or public accountant. A good accountant won't try to tell you if you have a good idea or not, that's what the market does when you try to create your first sale. But a good accountant will quickly help you see the financial implications of what your are about to do, and he will let you know if you need to talk with an attorney before your first sale.

It is best to start your first business doing something you know inside and out. This knowledge comes from your first-hand experience as a consumer or on the job. This intimate knowledge gives you the confidence to take action based on a hunch.

Phase III-Be in Business-Start-up!

Just do it!

You are in business once you have a passionate belief in an objective and set of goals that define what you are going to do for your future customers and what you want in return.

Usually the successful entrepreneur does not have a written plan beyond this simple objective and set of goals, what I call a strategic intention.

At startup, a full-blown, formal strategic plan is a handicap because: 1) writing it wastes time you could be using for selling and operations; and 2) you become a slave to the written plan and lose the entrepreneurs advantage-being able to rapidly adjust to the reality of the market on a daily basis.

I call the date you first have this strategic intention the Aha! Date for that business or project.

Each morning, plan your day based on the most current version of your strategic intention, your objective and goals. Make a list of the five most important things you can do that day to advance toward your objective. Every few days, review what you've accomplished, think about what the market is telling you, and revise your strategic intention. If you go in a new direction and change the objective, change your Aha! Date.

Sell Your First Customer as Quickly as Possible.

The successful entrepreneur combines analysis with action. Selling is always the primary job of the successful entrepreneur, from the first sale to the end of the entrepreneur's involvement with the business. Selling is pay-as-you-go market research. Write about what you learn in your journal.

Talk with your mentor, or find someone to mentor yourself. Now that you are in business, you may meet someone who recognizes the value of your fresh experience. Being a mentor is a great way to make what you have learned permanent. Share what worked, and share what did not work. Those who don't remember their mistakes are destined to repeat them.

Set Up a Business Checking Account.

After your first sale, set up a business checking account and deposit your first check. Hire a good CPA (and a good attorney if your CPA thinks you need one). Let them deal with the government for you, and make sure you understand fully what they are doing for you. Ask questions. Good accountants and lawyers are good teachers. But don't expect them to know whether or not your business idea is worthwhile, the market renders the final judgment.

Big time-wasters for the new entrepreneur during this start-up phase are the short seminars conducted by groups such as the SBA, SCORE, Small Business

Development Centers and Chambers of Commerce groups.

You may want to go to these seminars while you are preparing to go into business, and during the growth phase of your business. During start-up, you are much better off working directly with a good accountant. Guard your time carefully during this critical phase.

Form a Team of Advisors.

Eventually, you may want to form a board of directors (if a corporate business form was chosen by you and your accountant) or a group of advisors to help shift from the start-up to the growth phase of the business. The best group includes your accountant, attorney, and banker. You may want to continue working with your mentor, but only if it is clear that the work will continue to be of benefit to both of you.

You may also want to hire a sales consultant after your first sale or two. A good sales consultant will be able to help you convert what you've learned making your first sales into a polished system. The system will make sure you are working smart, and it can be used to duplicate yourself through other sales people.

Hire other specialists as needed to help you build a website, do advertising, get publicity, etc. Always have a clear understanding of what you will get, what it will cost, and when you will get it. It is usually a good idea to have this understanding in writing, which can just be a simple letter or memorandum that lists who is doing what.

Continue listening to what the market is telling you. Advisors can help you with the mechanics of your business, but they can never tell you how to best meet the needs of your market. No matter how much you tell your advisors, they will never know as much about your business as you do. Only you can see the complete picture, so only you can make the final decisions about your business.

Phase IV-Growth

After you have started, grow after tax profit as fast as you can, consistent with what you want. Businesses are like anything else in nature, they grow or they die.

Be ready to sell or abandon your business, especially your first business, if it is not meeting your needs. One entrepreneur who has started over twenty successful businesses told us at an IDEA Café that he knows it is time to sell when he stops having fun.

Do Just Enough Planning

Continue the process of having a clear objective and set of goals. Stay flexible. Expend the time and money to write a formal business plan in this phase only if:

* You are forced to raise capital from investors or lenders, or

* You have employees you do not directly supervise, or

* You want out and the plan will help you sell the business.

Large companies are forced to do formal, strategic planning. The fact that you do not have to waste time with this very time-consuming process is one of your biggest competitive advantages. You have a strategic planning conference each morning when you plan your day and review your objective and goals. Write down as little as possible, so it is easy to change direction quickly based on new information.

Reinvent Your Business to Keep It Growing.

All businesses eventually become mature and go into decline as new technology becomes available and new competitors come into the market.

Today this decline starts very soon after start-up for most businesses because of the incredible information/communications revolution we are experiencing. Reinvent your business by going through the Phase II-Preparation and Phase III-Startup steps again.

One way to get out of the rut and stimulate your own creativity is to go through these steps again yourself as you mentor a new entrepreneur.

Passing on your experience reinforces your own learning, and it is an invaluable source of information and inspiration for the person who is lucky enough to work for you.

Finding a new entrepreneur is not difficult. Friends or relatives will come to you once they learn you own and operate a business. Or, you may meet a new entrepreneur at the IDEA Café or other business organization.

Set a time to meet on a regular basis until he or she makes the first sale and forms a group of advisors which may or may not include you. On your first meeting, explain that you are agreeing to be a coach for your own benefit, to stimulate your own creativity and as a tool for your own learning.

Promise to share your experience as honestly as you can, to act as a sounding board, and to give encouragement not advice. Keep things very simple, and help the person find their own answers by being a good listener. Try to limit what you share to your own direct experience during the start-up of your business.

Hire a Potential Entrepreneur as Your Assistant.

Working with family, friends, and other potential entrepreneurs can be one of the great benefits of owning a business. If you don't have a family member you can work with, it's easy to find others.

Your assistant-to takes part of the burden of business details from your desk. This allows you to spend time training him or her and to reinvent your business. Limit time in the assistant-to position, from 6 to 18 months seems to be best. If your assistant-to isn't ready to launch at the end of that time, put him or her into a line position in your company.

Working together you both benefit: explaining your business helps you see it through fresh eyes; and the experience of working with an experienced entrepreneur is invaluable for your assistant.

My first job after graduate school was working as the assistant-to-the-president for an entrepreneur. Later, I taught the "Assistant-to Seminar" for the American Management Association with Victor Phillips, author of *The Organizational Role of the*

Assistant-to. (American Management Association, 1971)

Phillips had done his DBA on the Assistant-to after getting interested in it when he was teaching at the Air Force Academy. Using the assistant position for training is a very common practice in the military (aide de camp) and with some large organization.

You may want to make part of your assistant's compensation package help starting his or her own business. Maybe you can become his or her first customer. Or you can help by providing some of the capital for the first business in the form of a lump sum payment or gift (usually the best for both of you) or in the form of a loan.

Conclusion

Starting a new business is very simple, but success is very difficult.

Success depends primarily on character, personal resources, and making an endless series of difficult decisions quickly that result in effective action. Luck comes to the prepared.

Know when to pick a new direction (see Seth Godin's The Dip **http://sethgodin.typepad.com/the_d ip/**) and always do the work you love. The biggest problem with our society for the last 50 years has been retirement. The best and brightest too often cash out and die young. Humans are designed to wear out not rust out. Plan on constantly reinventing your work.

Follow your passion. Be open to all the possibilities. Maybe you will be led to work with the poor, run for political office, or teach small children. Your happiness and the welfare of society depend on you and me doing

something, even if we just own a
popcorn stand.

Appendix I-Creating New Customers

These ten steps are the fastest,
cheapest, most effective way I've
found to create the first new customer
for a new business.

They work even better for existing
businesses that just want one or more
GOOD customers to add to their
existing customer base.

Since 1980, I have designed and
implemented proactive selling systems
based on the basic approach with
hundreds of my consulting clients,
creating thousands of new customers
for them.

If you are just starting a new business, you need to be ready to do business with your first new customer before you use the process. If you are using the system described in this book then you're at Phase III-Be in Business-Start-up!

This system is very simple. The repetition is very persuasive. Good salespeople know that, given enough time, they can sell just about anything to just about anyone. The difference between a good, professional salesperson and a con artist is that the salesperson delivers what is promised!

The ten steps are not as glamorous as creating an advertising campaign; they are the infantry of selling. The steps will create customers for you the old-fashioned way, one at a time.

The process will also result in loads of valuable marketing information you

can use to fine-tune your objective
and goals and perhaps eventually use
to create an ad campaign. Good
selling is pay-as-you-go market
research.

**Step 1-Make Telephone Contact
with a Potential Prospect**

Running advertisements is expensive.
Direct mail to cold prospects is not as
effective as it once was. Networking is
just a waste of time without follow-up.

But a telephone call to a potential
prospect is powerful and cheap, if you
do it the right way. Be prepared and
be selective about who you are
calling, make ten calls, and it's
reasonable to expect at least one
good prospect.

In the past, you could often set an
appointment for a face to face meeting
on this first phone call. Today, that is

usually not possible no matter how good your product or service.

So settle for creating a good impression with this first phone call, sending more information (which is easier and faster than ever with email), and then making a second phone call to set the appointment.

Who do you call?

Make a list of 20 to 30 potential prospects. The best list comes from your personal address book, people you already know. Pick out those you suspect are most likely to need your product or service, and people who will want to help you find people to help.

If you don't find plenty of prospects from your personal address book and the people that are referred to you by your friends, you are probably going into the wrong business.

When calling your friends, ask for referrals. Having a direct relationship with the person you are calling warms up the call and takes off the heat from any telemarketing no-call rule, in my opinion. If you are in doubt, talk with your attorney.

If you need more names than you have from your personal address book and referrals, talk with the reference librarian at your local public library.

Tell the librarian about your product or service and who you are trying to reach. It is very likely that there is a directory with just such people. Eventually, you may want to buy a copy of the directory or a mailing list, but for your first few sales just copy the listings.

If you are calling businesses, there is no problem with telemarketing no-call rules. If you are calling consumers at home, you need to find a charity or political campaign to sponsor your call; don't bring up your business on the first contact, only be a volunteer for the charity or political campaign. If you are in doubt, see your attorney.

What do you say?

This first phone call is the most important step in this ten step process. You must have a great message and sound interesting. How? It depends on your market, your offer, your particular intention, you must be creative.

For this and every personal phone call for a business purpose, I suggest you use a script. The script is a powerful tool if it is well constructed and used correctly. It needs to be written to be heard, just as a radio commercial is written. You need to be a bit of an actor when using the script; a good actor never sounds like an actor! It is critical that you never sound like you are just reading from a script.

Practice with a friend or a tape recorder until you sound natural.

Creating well written scripts and developing the skill to use them is the best investment of time and money a new business owner can make. I have written hundreds of scripts. If you need help with this critical first step, give me a call and I'll send you a free copy of my special report "How to Write an Effective Script and How to Use It on the Telephone."

How many calls do you need to make?

When you get on a roll, keep calling! After you have found your first prospect and sent your first follow-up mailing, keep calling. The more prospects the better. Try for at least three appointments on your calendar before you go to your first face-to-face appointment.

If you can't find anyone who is interested, or if you can never seem to get around to making this first phone call, get some help from a sales coach. If you still can't find anyone who is interested, pick up your marbles. Take what you have learned and quickly go into another business.

Step 2-Send a Sales Letter to the Prospect:

In the past, you could start at this point and skip the first phone call. But today there is too much competition in the mail box; cold direct mail has lost its impact in most cases.

Send this mailing the same day you talk with the prospect on the telephone. The telephone call will be fresh in his or her mind when they get the letter, and that will make the letter seem personal. Nobody likes to get junk mail. Also, getting the letter out quickly demonstrates your competency to the prospects and builds their confidence in your abilities.

Your mailing does not have to be expensive, just a letter with a piece of sales literature. The letter sells, the sales literature tells what you do. With today's computers and inexpensive high quality printers it is easy to look good. The only limit is your imagination. If finding the right words is a problem, you may want to get professional help. Give me a call and if nothing else we can brainstorm on the telephone!

What is the best piece of sales literature? A photocopy of an article about your business from a newspaper or magazine. Your story in print is much more effective than a brochure with the same information. The publication sanctifies your story in most people's minds. But don't let trying for a news article and getting a brochure written and printed delay your phone calls. A simple typewritten flier will work for your first sale.

At the end of the sales letter, call for action. Ask the prospect to call you and set a time to meet. Realize that most won't call. The few who do are your best prospects. The others you call back later.

This follow up can be sent by fax or email, but some of the sales punch will be lost because the fax or email message will not have the same graphic appeal. But in some cases this loss of quality is more than made up for by the speed of your follow-up.

Step 3-Make a Second Phone Call to Set Appointment.

Most prospects will not call you, so after 14 days (if you mailed rather than using the fax or email follow-up) its time to start dialing. If you call sooner, many will not have had a chance to read your mailing. A premature follow-up call can scare off good prospects. You want to seem eager, not desperate.

When you call, don't ask if they received your mailing. If they did, great, it will help you on this call. If they didn't, or if they can't remember, asking about the mailing just creates a delay. On this second phone call the only goal is to get an appointment.

Just as with the first phone call, a good script and the ability to use the script so it doesn't sound like you are just reading is critical. If you'd like help with this, give me a call.

If you send a fax or email, call much sooner. Usually the next day is best.

Step 4-Send a Second Sales Letter to Confirm the Appointment.

Keep this letter short. Confirm the time of the appointment. Explain that the purpose of the appointment is for you to gather enough information to be able to determine if you can help. Include a second piece of sales literature. Perhaps you now have a news article about your new business to send.

Steps 5 and 6-Make Two Phone Calls to Confirm the Appointment.

Make two phone calls to confirm the appointment, one the day before, and again just before you leave for the appointment. Gather more information to further qualify the prospect. Reinforce the message from your sales literature. These phone calls demonstrate to the prospect that you are organized and eager to be of service. And they give you two more advertising impressions before your face-to-face meeting.

Step 7-Conduct Fact-finding Session.

It's best to meet with your prospects in their home or office for this first meeting. You get lots of information just by seeing them in their natural habitat.

Have a short "show and tell" about your product or service. I like to have an eight to ten page presentation in a three-ring binder. Use lots of pictures and graphics, people remember what they see much better than what they hear.

Then gather the information you need to make a proposal.

Before the fact-finding session, develop a list of questions for the prospect. You may want to have a standard questionnaire; believe-it-or-not, prospects never object to this and it makes you look more professional to most people. Or just use a yellow pad. Put whatever you use, take notes! You may also want to tape record the session with the prospects permission.

After gathering enough information, your sales message is "it sounds like I can really help you!" Suggest a second meeting, this time at your location. Even if you have a home-based business it may be best to meet the prospect on your turf for the Solutions/Presentation Appointment.

If your office is not suitable for this, borrow or rent a conference room. Depending on your product or service, you may be able to combine this fact-finding appointment with the solutions appointment for a one-call close (more about this in Step 10-Conduct a Solutions/ Presentation Session.)

Step 8-Confirm the Appointment by Letter.

Send another sales letter confirming the Solutions/ Presentation Appointment. Include a third piece of sales literature.

It is best if the letter goes into the mail the same day you meet with the prospect, following the fact-finding session you just conducted.

This can be a type written letter, confirming some of the information you gathered and setting up the solutions you anticipate presenting at your next meeting. But don't say anything about the actual solution; just stress the benefit of solving the problem and your confidence in being able to help.

A friend of mine worked for a well-known management consulting firm that targets the largest corporations in the world. As he and the senior consultant were leaving their prospects world headquarters after their fact-finding session with the board of directors, the senior consultant asked my friend, "Do you see what they should do?" Yes, my friend answered; the solution to their problem was obvious. "If we recommend, and the client implements, what will the profit impact be?" My friend gave his estimate. "Our take will be 25% of the profit, that amount divided by our average hourly rate gives us the number of hours we need to recommend to get to the solution we see now."

My friend could have sent the board the obvious solution in the appointment confirmation letter. His employer, the consulting firm, would have lost their fee. The client would have lost, too. Smart management consultants working with large firms know their clients buy consulting services they same way they buy nails, by the pound. Two months later the thick report confirming my friend's hunch gave the board the confidence to take action.

Step 9-Confirm the Appointment by Phone

Confirm the Solutions/ Presentation Appointment with a phone call the day before the appointment. Make sure the prospect has directions and that the time will work. Presell them on your solution.

If you need your potential client to bring something (like their check book) be sure to remind them.

Ask, "If you like what we present, is there anything that will prevent you from giving me a go-ahead to get started?"

If the prospect wants to talk with one of your competitors before making a final decision, try to reschedule so you can present after your competitor.

If the person you met with for the Fact-finding Session finally admits he or she will need to get approval from someone else before making a final decision, try to reschedule the appointment so the real decision maker will also be at the Solutions/Presentation Appointment. If possible try to set up an additional Fact-finding Session with the new final decision maker before you present your solution.

Step 10-Conduct a Solutions/Presentation Session

Develop a standard written solutions presentation and agreement for your product or service. Customize it for each prospect. Make it clear to the prospect that this solutions meeting is a working session by heading the proposal "DRAFT." Sit down with the prospect and read through the document line by line, correcting any errors and making changes and additions the prospect wants as you go.

Wait for the green light. The pressure to go forward should come from the prospect. It is best to leave prices blank until the agreement is finalized and the prospect has decided to go ahead if the price is right. If you sense the prospect is not ready to go forward, suggest that you make the corrections to the proposal and then meet at another time to review the changes.

Repeat this process until the prospect and you reach an agreement about how best to work together. After you've decided together what work you are to do, negotiate a price.

Given enough time eventually any prospect will buy from you. The question becomes, how much time are you willing to invest with the prospect before they write you your first check?

At some point (usually sooner than later) it is more profitable for you to decide to move on. Don't waste your time with people who are greedy and not willing to pay you what you are worth and what you need.

After reaching agreement, immediately send the new customer a "love letter" thanking him or her for their business and confirming what you have promised to do. Then deliver more than you've promised. Delight your new customer so he or she will give you repeat sales and referrals.

What's next?

After you've sold your first customer using this system, you may want to leverage your time through other people who help you with your selling. A good first step may be a part-time person to help you with the first phone call. I have worked with hundreds of my clients to help them do this, and it can quickly take your business to warp speed.

Far better is it to dare mighty things, to win glorious triumphs, even though checkered by failure... than to rank with those poor spirits who neither enjoy nor suffer much, because they live in a gray twilight that knows not victory nor defeat.
T. Roosevelt

Questions? Contact John S. Wren, MBA+, 960 Grant St. #727, Denver, CO 80203. John@JohnWren.com or call (303)861-1447.

This life is short, let's get started!